5 VERSES, 10 LESSONS

SPRINKLING POSITIVE VIBES

ADITYA P. PRADHAN

Copyright © Aditya P. Pradhan
All Rights Reserved.

This book has been self-published with all reasonable efforts taken to make the material error-free by the author. No part of this book shall be used, reproduced in any manner whatsoever without written permission from the author, except in the case of brief quotations embodied in critical articles and reviews.

The Author of this book is solely responsible and liable for its content including but not limited to the views, representations, descriptions, statements, information, opinions and references ["Content"]. The Content of this book shall not constitute or be construed or deemed to reflect the opinion or expression of the Publisher or Editor. Neither the Publisher nor Editor endorse or approve the Content of this book or guarantee the reliability, accuracy or completeness of the Content published herein and do not make any representations or warranties of any kind, express or implied, including but not limited to the implied warranties of merchantability, fitness for a particular purpose. The Publisher and Editor shall not be liable whatsoever for any errors, omissions, whether such errors or omissions result from negligence, accident, or any other cause or claims for loss or damages of any kind, including without limitation, indirect or consequential loss or damage arising out of use, inability to use, or about the reliability, accuracy or sufficiency of the information contained in this book.

Made with ♥ on the Notion Press Platform
www.notionpress.com

All those people who have been with me through my thick and thin are my inspirations behind writing this book. Mom, Dad, Shubham, Sarvesh and other friends, cousins, family, etc. Thank You!

Contents

Preface   *vii*

1. VERSE (1): ALWAYS REMEMBER   1
2. VERSE (2): LIFE IS EVERYTHING.   3
3. VERSE (3): NEVER GIVE UP!   4
4. VERSE (4): A TREE'S TIPS.   6
5. VERSE (5): WHEN YOU FEEL LIKE STOPPING   8
6. LESSON (1): LETTING GO OF NEGATIVITY   10
7. LESSON (2): HUNT FOR THE POSITIVES IN LIFE.   13
8. LESSON (3): FOCUS ON WHAT YOU WANT, NOT ON WHAT YOU DON'T.   17
9. LESSON (4): BELIEVE IN HAPPINESS IS A CHOICE!   20
10. LESSON (5): BE SOCIALLY ACTIVE.   24
11. LESSON (6): APPRECIATE, APPRECIATE & APPRECIATE!   28
12. LESSON (7): BELIEVE IN LOVE & HUMANITY ARE THE BEST THINGS.   30
13. LESSON (8): EXPLORATION IS THE KEY.   38
14. LESSON (9): IDOLIZE A FAMOUS PERSONALITY.   40
15. LESSON (10): NEVER STOP THIS PROCESS.   42

Preface

"If you're positive, you'll see opportunities instead of obstacles" -- This line made my mind stronger than ever. I am a great believer of the power positivity possesses and some of my experiences and feelings made me to write this book.

As I am writing this book amidst a global pandemic which has been active for more than a year now (started spreading rigorously since 2020), people now a days tend to be in somewhat a negative mind-space because of regular lockdowns, work from home, tension about career, future, health issues and many more things. The pandemic has eaten up many innocent lives till now, leaving behind their families helpless. Yet, with great courage and determination, many people managed to move forward to resume their life. My heart goes out to such people. But one thing which I observed closely is, those people who are mentally strong, and always carry a positive mindset, never fall prey to depression or unsuccessfulness. These times are tough. It is very obvious that each and every human is trying to get rid of continuously sitting at home, but alas, the situation outside is not allowing us to do so. So, in such situations, it is very important for all of us to stay calm, positive and think that *'It's just a matter of some time.'*

This book contains a mix of poems and lessons and aims exactly at eradicating negative-ness from the readers' minds and also, it's a small effort from my side to bring a ray of positivity in day-to-day life of those who reads this book. This book is for all those who are currently in a negative state of mind, not only for those affected by the pandemic (mostly all of us are) but also for those who are in a negative mind-space because of relationship issues, family matters, career tensions, etc.

Also, I'll advise that even if you are living your life on good and positive terms, you should read this book, as it will help you to improve and make yourself more better.

PREFACE

Not a very big one, but I feel after reading this, readers will definitely get to know how the power of a positive mindset works, and it will help them to grow as a good human in a phenomenal way.

CHAPTER ONE

VERSE (1): ALWAYS REMEMBER

You are the author of your own song,
So when the tune starts to feel wrong,
Don't reach for silence, don't end the play,
Pause, breathe, and try a new way.
Life isn't perfect, but it's still a gift,
A journey that gives, a quiet uplift.
Even in moments heavy and stark,
There's a flicker, a fire, a vital spark.
If you tell yourself you're bound to fall,
You might never rise at all.
But strength begins inside the soul,
A whisper that says, "I'm still whole."
You can choose the easy end,
Or gather your will and start to mend.
Even a faint flame in the night
Can grow into morning's light.
Don't close the book on a single page
Written in sorrow or silent rage.
Write on, with grit, with grace, with flame,
Let your triumph sign your name.
So take that step, no matter how small,
Stand through the stumbles, rise from the fall.
Your story is yours; bold and true,

And no one can live it but you.
— Aditya Pradhan

CHAPTER TWO

VERSE (2): LIFE IS EVERYTHING.

Life is a canvas, don't just watch, paint.
It's a storm, don't run, learn to dance in the rain.
It's a spark, nurture it till it lights your path.
It's a question, dare to ask, and then to act.
Life is a climb, not to escape, but to rise.
It's a mirror, look deep, not just at the surface.
It's a wound,yes, but one that teaches healing.
It's a chance, not once, but in every feeling.
Life is music, find your rhythm, lose your fear.
It's a maze, get lost, and you might find what's clear.
It's a whisper, soft, but full of power.
It's a seed, plant it with care, watch it flower.
Life is yours, not to borrow, not to waste.
Own each second, move with grace.
It's not about perfect, but being true,
And every heartbeat begins with you.

- Aditya Pradhan

CHAPTER THREE

VERSE (3): NEVER GIVE UP !

Don't quit;
Not when the night feels too long,
Not when doubt hums its cruel song.
Because the break you seek
Is often a heartbeat away.
Chase your dream like it's breath,
Like it's fire stitched into your chest.
Stay true;
To your choices, your path,
And the right that burns quietly in you.
Hold your vision like it's glass;
Delicate, but unshatterable in your hands.
Guard it from those
Who play false games
And write with disappearing ink.
Fuel your flame;
Others may never strike the match.
But you?
You are inches from the mark.
The world just hasn't caught on yet.
There's a chapter
That only you can write;
Where your name echoes

ADITYA P. PRADHAN

Like thunder wrapped in light.
Not even Oprah could predict it.
So don't vanish in the waiting.
Don't turn your back on your own becoming.
Never, ever
Give up on you.

— Aditya Pradhan

CHAPTER FOUR

VERSE (4): A TREE'S TIPS.

Grow tall; but not in pride,
Just in quiet strength.
Let your roots run deep
Into the soil of where you began.
Don't rush;
The sky isn't going anywhere.
Stretch with grace,
And let your stillness speak.
Hold your shape in every season.
Drop what no longer serves you.
Offer shade, not for praise;
But because someone may need it.
Drink in light,
Bend in storms,
And stand again without complaint.
You were never made
To bloom for applause.
You were made
To be true;
Even when no one is watching.
Remember where you came from.
Reach for what's above you.
And while you can;

ADITYA P. PRADHAN

Take in the view
   Called life.
                              - Aditya Pradhan

CHAPTER FIVE

VERSE (5): WHEN YOU FEEL LIKE STOPPING

There'll be days
When everything feels too loud,
And progress moves
Like footsteps through mud.
You'll climb hills
That weren't on the map.
You'll pay costs
That weren't in the plan.
And sometimes,
You'll smile only to stop the ache.
But don't close the chapter.
Rest if you must;
But don't erase the story.
Victory often hides
Behind the messiest moments.
The breakthrough doesn't shout;
It waits in silence,
Right after your patience wears thin.
So when your hands tremble
And your hope feels fake,
Stay.
Sometimes the finish line
Is just beyond the part

That made you want to quit.
- Aditya Pradhan

CHAPTER SIX

LESSON (1): LETTING GO OF NEGATIVITY

Letting go of negativity is the first step on the path towards happiness and fulfillment. Negativity has the proclivity to seep into our thoughts, quietly, in worst case scenarios we encounter in life. When something does not go as planned, in the case of human nature, even a minor roadblock can set off a metaphorical self-destructive bomb in the form of endless streams of negativity and hopelessness.

The below points define standing against boundless emptiness, deeply growing self hostility, and protecting all that is left. Worst case scenarios, encountering a little or endless load of despairious loops, be it school or work, scatterbrained aspirations, relationships left to rot in questioning emotions- these are bound to happen if negativity is not confronted.

1.Engage In Deep Thought

Celebrities have done the extreme with social media, sharing scathing remarks made by the public, for fun franchises showcasing the worst side of social media. Self ridicule is not the goal here, instead it serves as a unique way of proving how absolutely absurd and laughable those comments are. Try applying the same principle to ruminate by making those thoughts tangible. Even better, grab yourself a family member or a friend to showcase the wonder called sharing.

Remember: "Sharing is caring" applies to emotions too.

2. Laugh More, Worry Less

Laughter is one of the most underrated therapies. A lighthearted joke, a funny memory, or even watching a cartoon or comedy show can break the cycle of negative thinking. No matter how old you are, if something makes you laugh, it's worth your time. Laugh at a joke. Laugh at your own mistakes. Laugh simply because you can; it's how the soul resets.

3. Breathe, Stretch, and Reset

Yoga and deep breathing aren't just for yogis. Sometimes, three mindful breaths can do more than three hours of overthinking. I still remember being 14 and failing three consecutive exams. I was devastated until a relative introduced me to the calming power of yoga. Ever since, whenever my mind feels clouded, I return to the mat; or at least to the rhythm of my breath. Pause. Breathe in. Breathe out. Regroup.

4. Move Your Body, Change Your Mind

When you feel trapped in negative thoughts, don't sit still with them. Go for a walk. Stretch. Dance. Play a game. Move. Physical activity releases tension, improves mood, and shifts your mental focus toward the present. Even stepping out of your room can break the loop.

5. Empty Your Head on Paper

Journaling isn't just for happy memories. Write down what's bothering you; uncensored and raw. Set a timer for 10 minutes. Once you're done, tear up the paper. Discard the stress along with it. It's symbolic, yes; but it's also powerful.

6. Have a 'Go-To' Line

Your mind responds to repetition. That's why having a personal mantra or statement helps. Mine is:
"Let's do this. Not all things are easy. But not all things are impossible either."
Find a phrase that speaks to you and repeat it when your mind starts spinning into doubt. Train your thoughts like you'd train a muscle.

7. Replace Negative with Positive. Immediately

Your brain can only focus on one thought at a time. So, when a negative thought arises, replace it immediately with the opposite.

"I'll never succeed." → "I'm on the road to success."

"I'm not good enough." → "I'm becoming the best version of me."

Do it often enough, and the brain starts believing the positive over the negative.

8.Use the Power of Affirmation

Affirmations are not magic but they're mental discipline. When a recurring negative thought visits you, promise yourself this:

For every one negative thought, I will repeat a positive affirmation for two minutes.

"I am strong."

"I am enough."

"I am growing every single day."

Say it out loud. Say it often. And don't stop until the negative voice gets tired of being ignored.

Final Word:

This lesson isn't just for those struggling with negativity. It's for everyone. Because even the most positive minds need maintenance. So check in with yourself. Laugh. Breathe. Share. Move. Affirm. And most importantly, believe in your ability to rise above your thoughts.

Negativity is loud, but your willpower can be louder.

CHAPTER SEVEN

LESSON (2): HUNT FOR THE POSITIVES IN LIFE.

The second of the most crucial habits to develop for a meaningful life is to intentionally search for positives around you. Yes, search. Because even though positivity surrounds you, you must get into the habit of seeking it out consciously, particularly when things are not easy.

Positives don't necessarily have to be huge or life-altering. They are usually found in the smallest, most mundane moments. For example, simply observing a baby playing in your house or local area can immediately brighten your mood. Their innocence, laughter, and raw expressions can melt even the most serious of thoughts. In the same light, spending quality time with loved ones, catching up with a friend, singing a favorite song, dancing like nobody's looking, or simply pouring yourself into your passion, these aren't hobbies, they're therapy. They are natural mood boosters.

It's aptly said: the more you look at anything with a positive outlook, the greater your chances of success at it. Because your mind becomes your greatest asset.

Let me share a story that beautifully captures this idea. There was a girl named Seeta. Life tested her early; she lost her mother when she was just two years old. Raised in a slum by her father, she lived with limited means but unlimited values. Her father may not have had riches, but he enriched her life with ethics, courage, and an unshakeable belief in seeing the good in every situation.

That belief shaped her. Despite all odds, Seeta scored a brilliant 87% in her board exams. She dreamt of pursuing science, but lack of money forced her to choose Arts. Still, she remained undeterred. She won a scholarship but faced countless challenges in college; especially emotional ones. She was harassed by her peers, and the constant mental strain began to wear her down.

But rather than crack, she chose to shift her attention. She made a decision, to seek out the positives, no matter how tiny. She decided to put her energy towards making better friendships, trying sports, and remaining devoted to her education. She challenged herself to evolve. Step by step, she became stronger, more alive.

She worked hard. Her overall performance secured her admission in a prestigious college after 12th, in spite of economic constraints. Life kept putting obstacles in her path, but choosing to find light in times of darkness became her superpower. Seeta eventually passed the civil services exams, became an IAS officer, and also became a motivational speaker and an avid Bharatnatyam dancer.

Her odyssey is a reminder that one choice, to concentrate on the positive can alter your whole destiny.

And so, you may be thinking: "How do I begin to look for positives?" The secret is simply shifting, change your mind. When something hard comes along, our tendency is to think, "This is impossible. How will I ever do this?" But what if you turned that around and you thought instead, "Yes, this is hard, but it's not impossible. I will try it."

This change in mind works like a switch in our brain. Experiments and testimonials both indicate that when we go in with a positive approach towards anything, the chances of succeeding are multiplied many timessometimes up to 80%. Why? Because positivity energizes effort, and effort generates results.

Even on your worst days, break out of that state of mind. Take a walk. Chat with someone. You'll be amazed at how a five-minute real conversation can shift your mood. And if you're so fortunate as to have grand-parents still living, speak with them. Elders possess decades of experience. Their soothing presence and supportive words can imbue you with a sort of strength that's difficult to explain.

Another excellent method of staying positive is to identify a goal and move towards it. Keeping a target in mind keeps you motivated, disciplined, and committed. It exposes you to new experiences and new individuals, and these become stepping stones to learning more good about you. The skills you acquire along the way also tend to remain with you throughout life.

I'm going to share something personal here. I've learned that when I begin to move too quickly, speaking rapidly, analyzing everything, rushing through my meals or projects; stress builds up. I have no control over my mind, and negativity begins to take the reins. But when I take a slowdown, even for a few minutes, something magical occurs. I feel more at peace. My mind clears up. I begin to see solutions rather than issues. Just walking slower, talking softly, and being attentive allows me to reattach to what truly matters.

And when you start looking for these positives, don't stop there. Share them. Spread the light. Be the ray of hope to someone who's lost in darkness. Because what you give out has a strange way of coming back to you. Perhaps not immediately. Perhaps not from everybody. But it does come back, sometimes from the most unlikely places.

Also, keep in mind: the way you treat others, the way you think about them, and the way you react when they hurt; you form how you treat and think about yourself as well. So when you pick up someone else, you go up a little bit higher yourself.

So, go ahead. Search for that one positive thing in your day. Maybe it's a smile, a song, a compliment, or the fact that you even attempted. Search for the positives. Cherish them. Let them steer your way.

Because at the end of the day, life doesn't just happen to us; it responds to how we decide to look at it.

CHAPTER EIGHT

LESSON (3): FOCUS ON WHAT YOU WANT, NOT ON WHAT YOU DON'T.

Once you've worked on eliminating negativity and begun looking for positives in life, the next most powerful step is to narrow your focus; shifting your mindset to concentrate solely on what you truly want, instead of wasting your energy on things you don't. It might sound basic, but many of us unknowingly feed our minds with all the things we're trying to avoid. That, in turn, invites them into our lives.

Prioritizing what matters is the core of personal growth. Whether you're trying to rise from a rough patch or simply aiming for excellence, knowing what exactly you need in life, alongside what's not worth your attention, is absolutely essential. Our minds have the ability to be laser-focused. But the moment we allow distractions or unimportant things to creep in, our performance starts to suffer. Take academics for example: instead of stressing about failure or comparing yourself with others, shift your energy toward thinking how to improve, how to prepare better, how to crack that competitive exam or ace that semester. Remember, failure should be looked at only when it comes, so you can learn from it and not constantly imagined beforehand, which only invites anxiety.

Step one: Learn to control your thoughts. It's easier said than done, but even beginning to be aware of your thoughts can have a powerful impact. When your thoughts are scattered, your emotions follow suit. But when your mind is calm and centered, you gain clarity, and your ability to plan and act improves significantly. Life begins to unfold according to your intention rather than randomly. When we don't take charge of our thoughts, life feels like a rollercoaster: full of ups and downs we never consciously chose. But they're not random, they're a direct reflection of uncontrolled thinking.

Start by acknowledging what you don't want. This helps you contrast and define what you do want. Then, in a moment of realization, flip the switch. That's how change begins. We often call it a miracle, but in truth, it's the manifestation of intentional thought. If we're capable of manifesting unwanted situations by focusing on them, imagine the power we hold in creating the life we truly want.

This ability to think, to visualize, to choose, to redirect; is the miracle. When you train your mind to focus, the chaos within begins to settle. Instead of being tossed around by random, fleeting thoughts, you start to experience peace and intention. Controlled thinking leads to meaningful outcomes. Random thinking? Only confusion.

Step two: Start visualizing what you desire. Thoughts are not just passive but they're powerful. Sit down with yourself and clearly identify what you want to achieve. Once that's done, keep it fresh in your mind. Picture it often. The more you think about your goals, the more doors will begin to open. But this is crucial: while visualizing, don't let contradictory thoughts interfere. For instance, if you're going through a phase of sadness or self-doubt, address those feelings before embarking on your goal-setting. A clouded mind leads to blurred goals. You need clarity. You need conviction. Because any trace of doubt weakens your vision.

Remember, your outer world reflects your inner thoughts. Think clutter, and you'll attract chaos. Think beauty, and you'll start to experience it. But if you think beauty and immediately follow it with doubt, you're neutralizing the process. Your thoughts must align and remain consistent to bring about what you envision. The universe responds to specificity. So, think in detail. Imagine your goals down to the tiniest step; yes, even the last screw, the smallest gesture. Once you commit to this visualization, paths and opportunities will begin to align themselves.

Step three: Be the person you want others to be for you. This one often gets overlooked. It's easy to focus on how we're treated, but harder to turn the mirror toward ourselves. But the truth is, we receive what we give. Kindness, respect, and goodness travel in circles. When you treat others with generosity, like holding a door open, offering a warm smile, or simply not reacting harshly, you're not just spreading good energy; you're setting up your own return.

And this is not about being artificial or doing things with expectation. It's about building a life around values you'd want reflected back at you. If you want to live in a kind, supportive world, be kind and supportive first. That includes strangers, friends, and especially those who are hurting, because the way you treat others directly impacts how you see yourself, and in turn, how the world responds to you.

So, with all of this in mind, controlling your thoughts, visualizing your path, and practicing kindness, your ability to focus on what really matters gets stronger. You start ignoring the noise and tuning into your true priorities, whether it's academics, relationships, dreams, or self-growth.

Let this lesson be your anchor: Focus is your superpower. What you choose to fix your eyes on will grow. Prioritize wisely, and your life will follow in the direction you set, lifting you out of dark days and into the heights of what's possible.

CHAPTER NINE

LESSON (4): BELIEVE IN HAPPINESS IS A CHOICE!

Is happiness something we can choose? Absolutely. And many people experience it every single day by simply deciding to pursue it. But here's the truth: there's no one-size-fits-all formula. What sparks joy for one person may not work for another. Happiness is deeply personal, and truly it's up to us to define and nurture it.

There is immense power in recognizing that you are in the driver's seat of your happiness. Others: family, friends, coworkers can be part of your support squad, cheering you on. Yet they do not control how you feel. You do.

And yes, life often throws us curveballs, job losses, heartbreak, illness, or even times when it just feels like the world is upside down. In those moments, being told "happiness is a choice" can feel insensitive. But here's the secret: finding even a tiny spark, a comforting song, a familiar scent, a shared smile can become the anchor that guides you back to light. Knowing that you have an option, even when everything else seems broken, can be the lifeline that breaks your fall.

However, choosing happiness isn't easy. It doesn't come naturally to most of us. I've had to train myself. I know what it's like to feel weighed down by life's ups, and I've learned that no event, no accolade, and no external outcome deserves to define my mood. That's why I commit to happiness daily, even when it requires effort, or even professional support.

Many people mistakenly believe happiness will come only after success, a promotion, a milestone, or 1,000 Instagram likes. But science shows these are fleeting. Sure, those moments feel good; but they wear off. True, long-lasting happiness comes from consistent, purposeful effort, like training a skill.

So how do we build a strong happiness practice? Here are 11 tips I rely on:

1. <u>Cultivate Gratitude</u>

No matter how rough life gets, there's something good if you look for it; like a roof over your head, supportive people, or your own healthy body. List three positives each day in a gratitude journal. Studies show this habit increases optimism and reduces anxiety. Since I started writing down things I'm thankful for, I've noticed a real shift in my mindset.

2. <u>Reframe Your Thoughts</u>

Every time negativity sneaks in, consciously replace it. If you think, "This is impossible," follow up with, "I'll learn and grow through this." This habit rewires your thinking and primes your mind for positivity.

3. <u>Smile—Even When You Don't Feel Like It</u>

Buddhist teacher Thich Nhat Hanh once said, "Sometimes your joy is the source of your smile; sometimes your smile is the source of your joy." Science backs this too: smiling activates endorphins, serotonin, and dopamine, helping elevate your mood. I remember following MS Dhoni's example, he smiles through pressure. That calm confidence speaks louder than any words.

4.<u>Choose Kindness</u>

Generosity boosts your serotonin and gives a natural "helper's high." During the pandemic, I reached out often, helped friends solve tech issues, offered emotional support. Each act left me lighter, happier, and more connected.

5.<u>Prioritize Healthy Connections</u>

Research consistently shows that meaningful relationships are the strongest predictors of happiness . Interact with family, friends, and even friendly strangers. Stay clear of those who bring toxicity;

personally, distancing myself from negative influences has brought clarity and peace.

6. Practice Mindfulness Meditation

Just 10–15 minutes of mindfulness each morning can calm stress hormones and reduce rumination. I've seen how meditating, even briefly before an exam can sharpen focus and calm nerves.

7. Engage with Purpose

Humans thrive on meaning. Whether it's volunteering, gardening, or starting a small project, purposeful action fosters lasting contentment. The PERMA model underscores it: Positive emotion, Engagement, Relationships, Meaning, and Accomplishment.

8. Embrace Satisfaction, Not Comparison

In this hyper-online world, comparing ourselves can be a joy thief. My mom always taught me: "Be content with your own blessings." True peace comes from appreciating what you have, not chasing what everyone else displays.

9. Notice Your Benefits

When we pause and observe, blessings often overshadow problems. Whether we have health, safety, time with loved ones, or even a calm evening, there's always something worth cherishing.

10. Withhold Complaints

Rather than lashing out, pause and reclaim your calm. Choosing peace over criticism makes a moment of discomfort much less damaging; for yourself and others.

11. Use Your Strengths Every Day

We all have talents, big or small; that bring us fulfillment. Whether it's drawing, problem-solving, empathizing, writing, or building; acting in alignment with your strengths sparks joy and a feeling of living true to yourself.

Final Take:

Life may feel hard. Yet there's always a positive angle if you choose to look for it. Happiness is not a passive state, it's an ongoing, intentional practice. And though it takes awareness, effort, and sometimes help from others, it's also deeply doable.

So go ahead; start today:
Write your gratitude list.
Smile at someone; even yourself in the mirror.
Lift someone else up.
Reflect on your strengths and purpose.
Let go of comparisons.

Because every choice you make to build happiness is a step toward living deliberately, lovingly, and whole-heartedly.

CHAPTER TEN

LESSON (5): BE SOCIALLY ACTIVE.

When life gets too heavy on our minds or hearts, our first inclination is often to withdraw away from people, social media, or even from daily interactions. We need silence, somehow hoping that it will calm the tempest within. For some, such a withdrawal provides peace. For others, it intensifies the blackness. And though each person handles things in their own way, I firmly believe that remaining connected socially, particularly in difficult moments can serve as an unlikely lifeline.

I'm not telling you that you need to go to every function or smile on cue. But sometimes, sitting with someone and listening can restore some sense of normalcy. Having someone there, particularly someone who truly cares, can be a comfort when words fail.

I have had moments where I mentally wore myself out, but a good old-fashioned heart-to-heart with a friend brought me some sense. Simply talking out loud, not having to censor myself, was a huge relief. So I urge you: when the load becomes unbearable, don't bear it yourself. Speak. Share. You'll be amazed at how much healing starts just by talking.

That being said, I understand that being social isn't for every body. Some desire to connect, but hold back due to fear, anxiety, or simply feeling "too exhausted to attempt." If that resonates with you, relax. You're not alone, and there are tiny, little steps you can take to begin rebuilding those bridges.

Here are some ideas to assist you in gradually stepping into a more connected life:

1.Start Slow and Intentional
You don't have to dive into big groups. Start by reconnecting with one friend or loved one. Reach out, check in, or even just respond to that unread message. Keep it casual. Go at your own speed. The goal is progress, not pressure.

2.First Impressions Matter
When creating new relationships, particularly with strangers, pay attention to your energy. Smile warmly, take a genuine interest, and be kind. As comfort increases, you can make regular excursions or spontaneous get-togethers. Even traveling alone or taking dates alone can pick you up when you feel stagnant.

The key? Do things that bring you joy; whether that's a beach walk, a quiet coffee, or a loud concert. Choose connection, not obligation.

3.Listen to Connect, Not to Respond
Being well-listened to is the foundation of meaningful connection. Practice being fully present with someone when they speak. Put away your phone. Make eye contact. Nod, smile, stay curious.

Ask them:
What lights them up?

What are they passionate about?

What matters most to them?

Don't interrupt or deflect the conversation to yourself. People yearn to be heard and understood, and your present listening may be the best thing you can do for them today. You'll sense increased connection and satisfaction in return.

4. Compliment with Candor
Few words: "You were outstanding in that meeting," or "That shade is stunning on you"; have the power to open up warm, long-term connections. But one thing: be sincere. Only say it if you truly mean it.

5. Get Involved in Social Pastimes or Volunteer Activities
Want to move a step ahead? Get involved with like-minded people. It may be a book club, an NGO, or even an art workshop. I associated myself with a community of cricket writers, and not only did it make me grow as a person, but it also strengthened my social bonding.

Social pastimes naturally create opportunities for people to meet, you already share something in common. That may be a passion for animals, plants, books, or art. Strangers become acquaintances and, in some cases, close friends over time.

6. Talk to Strangers (Yes, Really!)
Greet your barista. Ask your coworker about their day. Engage in conversation in a painting class you always wished you could take. These little actions stretch your comfort zone and hone your social skills.

When I finally emerged from my shell, I found people more receptive than I had thought. All it took was a little "hello" to get something started.

7. Give Yourself Time
If you're struggling with social anxiety, shyness, or feeling

inadequate, know that building connections is a process. It doesn't happen overnight. Some fear is normal; but if it feels too overwhelming or persistent, it's okay to seek professional support. Social anxiety, generalized anxiety, or even depressive thoughts can create barriers, but those barriers can be worked through with help.

- Why Social Connection Matters?

Human interaction isn't just "nice to have"; it's essential for emotional well-being. It brings joy, relieves stress, and provides support. Isolation, on the other hand, can make our inner struggles feel even louder.

In fact, in moments of deep pain, many of us are vulnerable to making harsh, impulsive decisions. I've seen it, and I've felt it. But the presence of even one compassionate listener can make all the difference.

So, please don't keep it inside. Talk to someone. Message a friend. Show up at a community event. Or simply just get out and sit where people sit. You don't need to say anything. But being around an open, human space can change your head space, and remind you that you are not alone.

Final Take:
Being socially engaged is more than "having fun." It's about the choice of life, day after day, particularly when life gets tough. It's about connection, support, and those serendipitous moments of joy even in adversity. And it's about recalling: people need people.

CHAPTER ELEVEN

LESSON (6): APPRECIATE, APPRECIATE & APPRECIATE !

Well really, when you try to be a better human leaving all the negativity aside, one thing I would recommend you all to follow is appreciating more and more people, doesn't matter how small or big their work/achievement is. We have a tendency to take for granted all we have. We focus on what we want to change, rather than treasure what is good in our lives such as our health, our relationships, our ability to participate in sport, and our opportunity to receive a valuable education. Feelings of ungratefulness are cyclical.

We think, "If only such and such would change, we would be happier or more productive." When we finally receive what we wanted, we immediately focus on the next thing. We become desensitized to the everyday joys of life and all that is going well. Appreciation helps break the cycle of never being satisfied. It creates space to find stillness in the busyness of life.

I am an ardent sports fan, and since I had been associated with it quite a few times, one thing that sport taught me is 'Success is a process full of ups and downs.' And the same gets applied in our day-to-day life too. Appreciation turns obstacles into opportunities. Challenges present possibilities of growth. By welcoming the process of overcoming trials, you are able to approach the situation with positive mindset rather than a negative one.

Appreciation can bring abundance into your life. Demonstrating thankfulness for all things brings a positive atmosphere into your relationships, sport, school, and home. Showing others you appreciate them will raise their morale and increases their desire to work hard.
Being very honest, we all have a desire to feel valued. Expressing your gratitude for others and acknowledging their actions will encourage them. In work, sport, or school, the best practice to show your appreciation is frequently, immediately, specifically, and honestly. Appreciation is a free gift that goes a long way to enhance the lives of others.

Also take a note that by appreciating others, sometimes what you get in return is blessings. It's always better to earn blessings and showing some kindness towards anyone isn't it? Also, some of you may think that by appreciating others reduces or takes away something from us, but that's wrong. Appreciating anyone neither reduces our own values nor it takes away anything from us. It's just a daily gratitude which we as humans show to the ones who are growing and working very hard in their own field, and our good words sometimes fuel them up to do even more better. This also takes us to a positive state of mind and we also earn respect in return.

CHAPTER TWELVE

LESSON (7): BELIEVE IN LOVE & HUMANITY ARE THE BEST THINGS.

One of the most significant things to keep in mind when you are rising above a negative mind-space or attempting to be an improved human is that you should never lose hope and faith in humanity and love.

Mostly, people suffer heartbreaks when they are in love or when something has not happened according to their plan. Now, what follows these things is losing the faith in humanity and love. After such things, a person who has been going through this, stops believing in love and humanity. By that, sometimes, he/she may often seem rude because they are afraid of the same heart-wrenching thing to happen again. But does this really improve us?
The response is NO! In no way, not being human with anybody or losing hope in love makes you a better person.
Try not to be in that situation, also, I'll describe both the humanitarian and the love part in brief here.

There was a young lady named Ananya who was a school teacher in a small town. Daily on her commute to school, she noticed an old man sitting by himself on a bench in the park. He looked tired and lonely, and every day he wore a set of frayed clothes with a small bag slung across his shoulder. Ananya had a strong sympathy for him and would frequently wish that she could do something for him.

It was a rainy day when Ananya decided to go up to the man and speak with him. His name was Mr. Sharma. He explained to her that he had lost his family many years ago and had nowhere to turn. He lived by performing small odd jobs here and there, but life had been cruel to him. Hearing his tale, Ananya's heart wrenched, but rather than feeling despairing at how bad the world was, she felt energized.

She began going to Mr. Sharma every day, taking him food and clothes, and assisting him with his daily needs. Soon, some other teachers and neighbors followed her example. They all decided to create a small community group to assist not just Mr. Sharma but other elderly individuals and vulnerable people in the town.

With time, their community became more powerful and began to arrange free medical checkups, food collections, and workshops for seniors. The town began noticing the difference, individuals who had been ignored and forgotten were now treated with respect and compassion.

One day, when the local media visited to report their tale, Ananya stated: "I could have easily have ignored Mr. Sharma like everyone else did. But believing in people and humanity provided me hope and courage to take action. Yes, there are difficulties and disappointments, but kindness and faith in people can shift lives. When we open our hearts, we don't just assist others; we become kinder beings ourselves."

Now, what does this incident teach us? It teaches us that however deep and harsh your heartbreak may be, one should never lose the kind human inside them. Kindness, trust, affection are the values which define us as true humans and because of failure at one point, we should not be harsh towards those who are really in need. Rich or poor, anyone is eligible to be treated right. And when somebody is facing a difficult time, he/she should at least remember this by not treating anyone inhumanly, as your own small error can destroy your image as a person in the minds of others.

Now, what is Love? And how does not losing faith in the term LOVE enable us to develop as a human?
To begin with, the word LOVE, here, is not all about the couple relationship love kind of thing, but it is all about each and every thing you enjoy. Love can be towards a game, hobby, individual, parents, relatives, friends, food items, studies, animals or anything and everything in this world. The word LOVE has no limits.

But, most people tend to fall into negativity due to such breaks or sudden heartbreaks they earn from the things they love. Like if whenever a couple breaks up, both the guy and the girl usually fall into a very deep negative mindset which is extremely dangerous for them if not warned as early as possible. (In some situations, it is different) Those situations are the worst. At times, things can even reach up to a level where anybody of them has a tendency to commit suicide. It causes a very large loss which the members of the family and other relatives of the person have to endure without any wrong doing. In order to prevent such scenarios, I'll provide some suggestions from my end which I believe would surely help in curing you.

If you're ending a relationship, be respectful about how you break it off. Always consider how you'd want to be treated if you were in the same position.

Attempt to break up in a way that is respectful to the other but be truthful. Be frank and inform the other individual why the relationship is ending. Realize that the other individual could be upset and perhaps angry over your choice.

Attempt to break up in person if possible and not via text or the internet.

Well, you have to be really careful in dealing with yourselves after a breakup, because one wrong choice will have its severe effects on you and your other loved ones. So, first of all, if issues are tiny and if there exists somewhere a hope of issues getting sorted out, then go for it. Before you move on, attempt that one chance of getting back together, or at least try it out. Don't hurry. Slow a bit, take some time out, and let your partner do the same. When you both feel it's the right time to discuss, if the issues get sorted out, it's good and well, and get back together and don't repeat the errors which prompt you to split at a particular point. But, if the reverse happens, it is but natural to grieve, but you can't do anything else if your partner wants to leave. Keep in mind, everything and anything that occurs within this world happens for a reason and it's entirely dependent on what's in your fate. Set them free. You can't coerce any decision from anyone and no one can coerce it on you as well. Just, remain calm, and prefer meditation after such incidents. Analyze yourself and instead of asking yourself "Am I so bad?", speak to yourself : "I am still strong and worthy." At such times, it is extremely necessary not to let your mental peace degrade to such a level where you're compelled to make any strict decision. After any sort of breakup, rather than getting lost in the past, get invested in new hobbies, new things, any cooking classes, courses and so much more. Try to keep yourself distant from that thing which provides you with negative vibes.

Take a step ahead outside that and observe how beautiful and opportunistic the world is. Even, make a good connection with new individuals and introduce yourself to new learnings and culture so that you will be mentally healthy all the time. Keep yourself occupied. You may have too much leisure time to yourself, particularly on weekends. Plan in advance and do activities that you normally like. Give yourself time. Do activities that relax you, such as watching a film, playing or listening to music, meditating, reading or sports. Talk to family and friends and other people who can offer you support. It is acceptable to need some time on your own but socializing with understanding people gives your mind a break from things, and gives you another outlook. Avoid using alcohol and other drugs to cope with the hurt. Although they may make you feel good initially, the consequences will make you feel ten times worse. Give it time.

Let yourself get used to the adjustment after a break-up. Additionally, having enough sleep and exercise is of utmost importance. Don't forget to allow your feelings to surface. Cry, sob your eyes out, scream and yell. As long as it doesn't injure yourself or anyone else, find ways to release and let go of the pain you might be experiencing. When people offer kindly and jokingly that all break ups are tough, it's because they are. Don't deprive yourself of this part of the healing process or else it will bud and ferment in you. You will inevitably feel some negative emotions regardless of how easy or difficult your break up was. Honour your feelings and recognize that they will become less intense the more that you release them. It helps you move forward from them! Listen to sad songs. Largely, listening to sad songs actually makes you happier. Listening to sad songs can manage negative emotion and mood as well as consolation.

Go somewhere quiet, let your feelings pour out, and provide yourself with some relief. And most importantly, it is most crucial to FIND YOURSELF and prioritize YOUR THOUGHTS more. You lost a part of yourself in this relationship. Now is your time to rediscover yourself and this can be enjoyable. This is one of the positives to your break-up, so go for it! Perhaps you gave up a hobby that you enjoyed or quit bathing in scented soap. You can have salad and granola bars for supper if you wish. There are plenty of personal things which made you unique, you only need to discover

them again and get the sensation back. On the other hand, you might have developed in the relationship so you can learn things about yourself. Take a thoughtful talk with yourself and undertake a thorough discovery into your inner-self.
Asking question questions can assist you in knowing more about yourself and what you really want to be.

Some possible questions you can ask:

If "love myself more" is the foremost virtue in my life, would I continue doing what I am doing presently to make it happen?

What do I value myself the most?

How was my life prior to the relationship?

What is it that I want in my life and how would I begin?

What is the foremost thing which I must improve?
The search for yourself is tough since most of us don't even have time to simply sit down and reflect on what we really want. It may take a long while, but you can take your own time doing so because it's so valuable! As you move on in your life, do not deny or cling onto the memory of your ex. They might come into your head as a memory of a time that you were glad (or not). Own it, smile or cry. Release the memory rather than holding on. Don't consciously look at photographs or glance at old messages you received from him. It's about you now and your current moments. Your ex is part of who you are today and you can be thankful to them for it, but the chapter with them is closed.

As stated earlier, CLEAR OUT everything that stirs up memories. Do not try to get away with your emotions. Confront them. Write down what you feel to clear your mind. The more that you write, the better you can recognize what provokes your emotion and you can prepare yourself better for them. Another thing here I would mention is Understand the beauty of being single and don't rush into another relationship. Don't bounce into another relationship too quickly, thinking that you're okay. It is most likely the best short-term solution around but meanwhile, you never really move past your ex. Down the road you haven't really moved past your ex and when your subsequent relationship ends, you'll have two ex's to move past. You're just delaying the pain. Ask yourself what you want in a relationship.

Know your need prior to entering into a relationship because this can save you from yet another heartbreak. Get to know new people and explore when you are ready. Ensure you communicate with them, spend enough time to understand them before making the leap to pursue a new relationship. And ultimately, plunge into a present life. It's nice to gradually and slowly cultivate a mindful life so your mind can remain peaceful and calm irrespective of what life brings you.

To be mindful is to listen to yourself more and recognize your need above all, get to know what can make you happy. Now, the other kind of LOVE is the affection which we have for a specific sport, animal, hobby or anything else. At times, it so occurs that we might not succeed in our dearest sport, or our dearest pet dies or is lost, or anything else which completely goes against what we believe. Yes! They hurt. No doubt. But, there exists a means to cross all these obstacles, and look towards a new tomorrow. Try to take one more attempt in your preferred area, bring home a new pet and make him feel much better, give increasing and increasing attention to things you love, instead of sitting, thinking and weeping about what happened earlier and is not available now.

Instead, do things which are still in your access, and have faith in the power of LOVE and Confidence. So, here I end this lesson, by stating that have faith in the power of LOVE & Humanity. Every thing occurs for a reason, and success lies behind every unsuccessful thing. Make an attempt to find out that. Due to one or two failures, don't allow the good human within you die. Don't allow your belief in love be out of sight. Strive to get involved with lots of interesting things rather than weeping over what has already passed away. Exhibit to the world what you are composed of, and motivate others undergoing the same experience to remain calm, have faith in the religion of humankind and love, and look at how lovely things around you will be.

CHAPTER THIRTEEN

LESSON (8): EXPLORATION IS THE KEY.

It is often said that nothing is better than exploring the world rather than staying stuck in the past. And I suggest you all do the same. The next step is to explore, not just the world, but yourself; instead of constantly replaying negative events over and over in your mind. This advice isn't just for those battling negativity; it's for anyone who truly wants to grow into a better version of themselves.

Exploration here means discovering yourself as much as discovering the world around you. I firmly believe that by exploring yourself, you prepare better for the challenges and goals ahead, rather than moving forward without a plan. The more you try, the more you'll learn about your likes, dislikes, strengths, and weaknesses, because these are uniquely yours!

As you explore, you'll figure out who you really are and who you want to become. Even if you think you already know yourself well, putting yourself in new situations always teaches you something new. After all, you never really know until you try, right?

Pushing ourselves out of our comfort zones is actually beneficial. Exploring new things helps us overcome fears and expands our minds by teaching us not only about the new experiences but also about ourselves.

Now, I'm not saying you need to jump out of a plane or try flying trapeze (though I wouldn't discourage it!). Getting out of your comfort zone doesn't have to be extreme. Even small steps like trying Acro-Yoga or learning a new skill you've always wanted to can feel like soaring high in the sky.

Let me share my own example. Before the pandemic, I was pretty lazy, mostly playing video games (I still do, but less now) and hardly reading books or novels. The pandemic made me realize there was so much more to explore and invest in. I always knew I could write and speak well on various topics because I had good command over language and ideas. So, I decided to write books. This journey has been wonderful; it brought me peace and happiness, and I'm proud to be successfully exploring and trying new things.

As I mentioned briefly in the previous chapter, every time you put yourself in a new situation, you challenge your brain to quickly understand unique circumstances, figure out how to handle them, and develop new skills. In other words, you're training your brain to be creative and solve problems every time you try something new.

For example, if you try gardening for the first time, your brain works in a brand-new way. Even if gardening isn't new for you, trying a new plant like beets introduces a unique set of rules and your brain will creatively find ways to succeed.

The possibilities are endless when it comes to trying or exploring something new. Whether it's a big leap or a small step outside your comfort zone, you'll still reap the benefits. So, join a group, go on a solo adventure, meet new people, learn a new skill, broaden your horizons, and give your soul a boost.

CHAPTER FOURTEEN

LESSON (9): IDOLIZE A FAMOUS PERSONALITY.

The best is to idolize or look up to a well-known celebrity or personality. Through this, we attempt to mimic what they did in their life so that we could become successful. In the past, humans worshipped and idolized gods. They constructed temples and statues for the gods, and worshipped them. They were their idols, to whom they prayed. Much time has since lapsed, yet the desire to worship and idolize has not lapsed, merely the idols and gods have evolved. They now refer to them as celebrities.

Celebrities are not created by nature; they are created. Sometimes their popularity is very short-lived, and sometimes, if they are good, their popularity may endure for a while. There are many reasons why we follow, adore and want to know more about people, whom we refer to as celebrities.

Now I will be writing about myself. I am a very die-hard follower of **MS Dhoni, the ex-Indian cricket team captain.** I admire him regularly, for by doing so, I have more reasons to live a good life. His on and off field approach, his composed nature and plain behavior, clever mind, and lots of other things motivate me to be a good human being. I always make an effort to be like him, and I attempt to enhance my personality looking at his. The way he deals with success and failures, motivates me the most. He has taught me a great deal in his career, and always will be my idol. My life has become quite cool and good since I was following him because since then I attempt to use the lessons that I receive from watching any of his events in my own life. Also, whenever I feel depressed, I simply switch on YouTube and see any of his innings or interviews, and that energizes me to return to normalcy.

Thus, in your life also, try to imbibe any celebrity, as it will surely assist in character development. Now, it can be anybody, politicians, sportsmen, actors, etc. When you watch their lives, interviews, or their biography, reading their own autobiography; will energize you to work and move forward in your life with more confidence and you can visualize yourself better in just days. Celebrities are human beings, just like any one else. They have their highs and lows, fears and joyful times, success and failure, like "normal" people.

Before I close this, I must note that we don't idolize and worship all celebrities. There are some who we don't like and don't want to know about. There are also individuals, who don't need so much to idolize and know about such personalities. They don't need that.

Also, lastly, I would say that sometimes, some individuals do idolize their parents, family members, friends, or any ordinary person around them who is performing exceptionally well in their own life, and that puts a tremendous impact on their mind. It sometimes actually works to admire "Normal People" rather than celebrities, because due to glamour, sometimes, the core motive gets lost.

So, even if you're worshipping any '**Ordinary Person**' within your reach, fine! It really will make you better in a more intimate and productive manner, but of course, get inspired by the positives and not the negatives.

CHAPTER FIFTEEN

LESSON (10): NEVER STOP THIS PROCESS.

This book may not be very long, but I truly hope that after reading it, you've understood the real power of positivity.

Being rich doesn't always mean having a fat bank balance. If you see a big smile on your mom or dad's face when they wake up, that's richness. If you have someone who knows just how to cheer you up when you're down, that's richness. If your friends call or message you right away when they sense something's off, that's richness. If you're doing something you love every single day; whether it's a hobby, a passion, a job, or a business that makes you rich. And most importantly, if you're happy, then you're the richest person alive. So stop putting a number on everything and start feeling rich with whatever you have right now.

Emotions are what make us human. So how can you just "overcome" them? If you do, you'll become stone-hearted; not just to others, but to yourself too. Instead of trying to crush your emotions, learn to control them and use them in the right place, where they matter and are appreciated.

Stress won't solve anything. If you want solutions, first be calm. Be patient. Believe in yourself, trust in some higher power, and think carefully about the keys to unlock your life's challenges. Keep trying until you find the right one.

There are three bonds that are unbreakable:
Your bond with yourself.

Your bond with your parents.
Your bond with God.

Sure, you'll feel low sometimes. But don't let negative thoughts push you toward negative actions or drain your energy constantly. Take control of your mind. You have the strength. Stop yourself with deep breaths and quickly switch your focus to something that brings you relief, whether it's self-care, talking to someone who lifts you, learning something new, going to a movie, exercising, or anything else that helps. Yes, it's hard but it's not impossible.

This book is my small attempt to sprinkle some positive vibes. I believe no one should get lost in the sea of negativity. Everyone deserves a happy, peaceful, and positive life. This book isn't just for those facing tough times; even if everything in your life is going well, I hope it gave you new lessons to add to your personal growth.

And please, share this book with your loved ones, and with anyone you think really needs to fight off negativity. After all, sharing is caring. Sharing positivity doesn't take anything away from us; it only brings us more respect and joy.

Made in the USA
Monee, IL
03 May 2026

49437776R00031